Lysander Spooner

A New Banking System

The Needful Capital for Rebuilding the Burnt District

Lysander Spooner

A New Banking System
The Needful Capital for Rebuilding the Burnt District

ISBN/EAN: 9783743404731

Manufactured in Europe, USA, Canada, Australia, Japa

Cover: Foto ©Suzi / pixelio.de

Manufactured and distributed by brebook publishing software
(www.brebook.com)

Lysander Spooner

A New Banking System

A

NEW BANKING SYSTEM:

THE

NEEDFUL CAPITAL FOR REBUILDING THE BURNT DISTRICT.

By LYSANDER SPOONER.

BOSTON:

SOLD BY A. WILLIAMS & CO.

135 WASHINGTON STREET.

1873.

Printed by
WARREN RICHARDSON,
112 Washington St

CONTENTS.

The reader will understand that the ideas presented in the following pages admit of a much more thorough demonstration than can be given in so small a space. Such demonstration, if it should be necessary, the author hopes to give at a future time.

Boston, March, 1873.

CHAPTER I.

A NEW BANKING SYSTEM.

Under the banking system—an outline of which is hereafter given— the real estate of Boston alone— taken at only three-fourths its value, as estimated by the State valuation*— is capable of furnishing three hundred millions of dollars of loanable capital.

Under the same system, the real estate of Massachusetts — taken at only three-fourths its estimated value†— is capable of furnishing seven hundred and fifty millions of loanable capital.

The real estate of the Commonwealth, therefore, is capable of furnishing an amount of loanable capital more than twelve times as great as that of all the "*National*" Banks in the State‡; more than twice as great as that of all the "National" banks of the whole United States ($353,917,470) ; and equal to the entire amount ($750,000,000, or thereabouts) both of greenback and "National" bank currency of the United States.

---

* By the State valuation of May, 1871, the real estate of Boston is estimated at $395,214,950.

† By the State valuation of May, 1871, the real estate of the Commonwealth is estimated at $991,196,803.

‡ The amount of circulation now authorized by the present "National" banks of Massachusetts, is $58,506,686, as appears by the recent report of the Comptroller of the Currency.

1

It is capable of furnishing loanable capital equal to one thousand dollars for every male and female person, of sixteen years of age and upwards, within the Commonwealth; or two thousand five hundred dollars for every male adult.

It would scarcely be extravagant to say that it is capable of furnishing ample capital for every deserving enterprise, and every deserving man and woman, within the State; and also for all such other enterprises in other parts of the United States, and in foreign commerce, as Massachusetts men might desire to engage in.

Unless the same system, or some equivalent one, should be adopted in other States, the capital thus furnished in this State, could be loaned at high interest at the West and the South.

If adopted here earlier than in other States, it would enable the citizens of this State to act as pioneers in the most lucrative enterprises that are to be found in other parts of the country.

All this capital is now lying dead, so far as being loaned is concerned.

All this capital can be loaned in the form of currency, if so much can be used.

All the profits of banking, under this system, would be clear profits, inasmuch as the use of the real estate as banking capital, would not interfere at all with its use for other purposes.

The use of this real estate as banking capital would break up all monopolies in banking, and in all other business depending upon bank loans. It would diffuse credit much more widely than it has ever been diffused. It would reduce interest to the lowest rates to which free competition could reduce it. It would give immense activity and power to industrial and commercial enterprise. It would multiply machinery, and do far more to increase production than any other system of credit and currency that has ever been invented. And being furnished at low rates of interest, would secure to producers a much larger share of the proceeds of their labor, than they now receive.

All this capital can be brought into use as fast as the titles to real estate can be ascertained, and the necessary papers be printed.

Legally, the system (as the author claims, and· is prepared to establish) stands upon the same principle as a patented machine ; and is, therefore, already legalized by Congress ; and cannot, unless by a breach of the public faith, any more be prohibited, *or taxed*, either by Congress or this State, than can the use of a patented machine.

Every dollar of the currency furnished by this system would have the same value in the market as a dollar of gold; or so nearly the same value that the difference would be a matter of no appreciable importance.

The system would, therefore, restore specie payments at once, by furnishing a great amount of currency, that would be equal in value to specie.

The system would not inflate prices above their true and natural value, relatively to specie ; for no possible amount of paper currency, every dollar of which is equal in value to specie, *can* inflate prices above their true and natural value, relatively to specie.

Whenever, if ever, the paper should not buy as much in the market as specie, it would be returned to the banks for redemption, and thus taken out of circulation. So that no more could be kept in circulation than should be necessary for the purchase and sale of property at specie prices.

The system would not tend to drive specie out of the country; although very little of it would be needed by the banks. It would rather tend to bring specie into the country, because it would immensely increase our production. We should, therefore, have much more to sell, and much less to buy. This would always give a balance in our favor, which would have to be paid in specie.

It is, however, a matter of no practical importance whether the system would bring specie into the country, or drive it out; for the volume and value of the currency would be substantially unaffected either by the influx or efflux of specie. Consequently industry, trade, and prices would be undisturbed either by the presence or absence of specie. The currency would represent property that could not be exported; that would always be here; that would always have a value as fixed and well known as that of specie; that would always be many times more abundant than specie can ever be; and that could always be delivered (in the absence of specie) in redemption of the currency. These attributes of the currency would render all financial contractions, revulsions, and disorders forever impossible.

The following is

An Outline of the System.

The principle of the system is that the currency shall represent an *invested* dollar, instead of a specie dollar.

The currency will, therefore, be redeemable by an *invested* dollar, except when redeemed by specie, or by being received in payment of debts due the banks.

The best capital will probably be mortgages and railroads ; and these will very likely be the only capital which it will ever be expedient to use.

Inasmuch as railroads could not be used as capital, without a modification of their present charters, mortgages are probably the best capital that is immediately available.

Supposing mortgages to be the capital, they will be put into joint stock, held by trustees, and divided into shares of one hundred dollars each.

This stock may be called the Productive Stock, and will be entitled to the dividends.

The dividends will consist of the interest on the mortgages, and the profits of banking.

The interest on the mortgages should be so high — say six or seven per cent — as to make the Productive Stock worth ordinarily par of specie in the market, *independently of the profits of banking.*

Another kind of stock, which may be called *Circulating Stock*, will be created, *precisely equal in amount to the* Productive Stock, and divided into shares of *one dollar each.*

This *Circulating Stock* will be represented by certificates, scrip, or bills, of various denominations, like our present bank bills — that is, *representing one, two, three, five, ten, or more shares, of one dollar each.*

These certificates, scrip, or bills of the *Circulating Stock,* will be issued for circulation as currency, as our bank bills are now.

In law, this *Circulating Stock* will be in the nature of a lien on the PRODUCTIVE STOCK. It will be entitled to no dividends. Its value will consist, *first,* in its title to be received in payment of all dues to the bank; *second,* in its title to be redeemed, either in specie on demand, or in specie, with interest from the time of demand, before any dividends can be made to the bankers; and, *third,* in its title, when not redeemed with specie, to be redeemed (in sums of one hundred dollars each) by a transfer of a corresponding amount of the capital itself; that is, of the PRODUCTIVE STOCK.

The holders of the *Circulating Stock* are, therefore, sure, *first,* to be able to use it (if they have occasion to do so) in payment of their dues to the bank; *second,* to get, in exchange for it, either specie on demand, or specie, with interest from the time of demand; or, *third,* a share of the capital itself, the PRODUCTIVE STOCK; a stock worth par of specie in the market, and as merchantable as a share of railroad stock, or government stock, or any other stock whatever is now.

Whenever PRODUCTIVE STOCK shall have been transferred in redemption of *Circulating Stock,* it (the PRODUCTIVE STOCK) may be itself redeemed, or bought back, at pleasure, by the bankers, on their paying its face in specie, with interest (or dividends) from the time of the transfer; and *must* be so bought back, before any dividends can be paid to the original bankers.

The fulfilment of all these obligations, on the part of the bank, is secured by the fact that the capital and all the resources of the bank are in the hands of trustees, who are legally bound — before making any dividends to the bankers — to redeem all paper in the manner mentioned; and also to buy back all PRODUCTIVE STOCK that shall have been transferred in redemption of the circulation.

Such are the general principles of the system. The details are too numerous to be given here. They will be found in the "*Articles of Association of a Mortgage Stock Banking Company*," which the author has drawn up and copyrighted.

CHAPTER II.

SPECIE PAYMENTS.

Although the banks, under this system, make no absolute promise to pay specie *on demand*, the system nevertheless affords a much better *practical* guaranty for specie payments, than the old specie paying system (so called); and for these reasons, viz:

1. The banks would be so universally solvent, and so universally known to be solvent, that no runs would ever be made upon them for specie, through fear of their insolvency. They could, therefore, maintain specie payments with much less amounts of specie, than the old specie paying banks (so called) could do.

2. As there would be no fears of the insolvency of the banks, and as the paper would be more convenient than specie for purposes of trade, bills would rarely be presented for redemption — otherwise than in payment of debts due the banks — except in those cases where the holders desired to invest their money; and would therefore *prefer* a transfer of PRODUCTIVE STOCK, to a payment in specie. If they wanted specie for exportation, they would buy it in the market (with the bills), as they would any other commodities for export.* It would, therefore, usually be only when they wanted an investment, and could find none so good as

* There would always be a plenty of specie for sale, in the seaports, as merchandise.

the PRODUCTIVE STOCK, that they would return their bills for redemption. And then they would return them, not really for the purpose of having them redeemed with specie, but in the hope of getting a transfer of PRODUCTIVE STOCK, and holding it awhile, and drawing interest on it.

3. The banks would probably find it for their interest, as promoting the circulation of their bills, to pay, at all times, such *small* amounts of specie, as the public convenience might require.

4. If there should be any suspensions of specie payments, they would be only temporary ones, by here and there a bank separately, and not by all the banks simultaneously, as under the so called specie paying system. No general public inconvenience would therefore ever be felt from that cause.

5. If the banks should rarely, or never, pay specie *on demand*, that fact would bring no discredit upon their bills, and be no obstacle to their circulation at par with specie. It would be known that — unless bad notes had been discounted — all the bills issued by the banks, would be wanted to pay the debts due the banks. This would ordinarily be sufficient, of itself, to keep the bills at par with specie. It would also be known that, if specie were not paid *on demand*, it would either be paid afterwards, with interest from the time of demand; or PRODUCTIVE STOCK, equal in value to specie in the market, would be transferred in redemption of the bills. The bills, therefore, would never depreciate in consequence of specie not being

2

paid *on demand;* nor would any contraction of the currency ever be occasioned on that account.

For the reasons now given, the system is practically the best specie paying system that was ever invented. That is to say, it would require less specie to work it; and also less to keep its bills always at par with specie. In proportion to the amount of currency it would furnish, it would not require so much as one dollar in specie, where the so called specie paying system would require a hundred. It would also, by immensely increasing our production and exports, do far more than any other system, towards bringing specie into the country, and preventing its exportation.

If it should be charged that the system supplies no specie for *exportation*; the answer is, that it is really no part of the legitimate business of a bank to furnish specie for exportation. Its legitimate business is simply to furnish credit and currency for home industry and trade. And it can never furnish these constantly, and in adequate amounts, unless it can be freed from the obligation to supply specie on demand for exportation. Specie should, therefore, always be merely an article of merchandise in the market, like any other; and should have no special — or, at least, no important — connection with the business of banking, except as furnishing the measure of value. If a paper currency is made payable in specie, *on demand,* very little of it can ever be issued, or kept in circulation; and that little will be so irregular and inconstant in amount as to cause continual and irremediable derangements.

But if a paper currency, instead of promising to pay specie *on demand*, promises only an alternative redemption, viz: specie on demand, or specie with interest from the time of demand, or other merchantable property of equal market value with specie — it can then be issued to an amount equal to such property; and yet keep its promises to the letter. It can, therefore, furnish all the credit and currency that can be needed; or at least many times more than the so called specie paying system ever did, or ever can, furnish. And then the interest, industry and trade of a nation will never be disturbed by the exportation of specie. And yet the standard of value will always be maintained.

The difference between the system here proposed, and the so called specie paying system — in respect to their respective capacities for furnishing credit and currency, and at the same time fulfilling their contracts to the letter — is as fifty to one, at the least, in favor of the former; probably much more than that.

Thus under the system now proposed, the real estate and railroads of the United States, at their present values, are capable of furnishing twenty thousand millions ($20,000,000,000) of paper currency; and furnishing it constantly, and without fluctuation, and every dollar of it will have an equal market value with gold. The contracts or certificates comprising it, can always be fulfilled to the letter; that is, the capital itself, (the PRODUCTIVE STOCK,) represented by these certificates, can always be delivered, *on demand,* in redemption of the certificates, if the banks should be unable to redeem in specie.

On the other hand, it would be impossible to have so much as four hundred millions, ($400,000,000) — one fiftieth of the amount before mentioned — of so called specie paying paper currency; that is, a paper promising to pay specie *on demand; and constantly able to fulfil its obligations.*

It is of no appreciable importance that a paper currency should be payable *on demand* with specie. It is sufficient, if it be payable *according to its terms, if only those terms are convenient and acceptable.* For then the value of the currency will be known, *and its contracts will be fulfilled to the letter.* And when these contracts are fulfilled to the letter, then, *to all practical purposes, specie payments are maintained.* When, for example, a man promises to pay wheat, either on demand, or at a time specified, and he fulfils that contract to the letter, *that, to all practical purposes, is specie payments;* as much so as if the promise and payment had been made in coin. IT IS, THEREFORE, THE SPECIFIC AND LITERAL FULFILMENT OF CONTRACTS, THAT CONSTITUTES SPECIE PAYMENTS; AND NOT THE PARTICULAR KIND OF PROPERTY THAT IS PROMISED AND PAID.

The great secret, then, of having an abundant paper currency, and yet maintaining all the while specie payments, consists in having the paper represent property — like real estate, for example — that exists in large amounts, and can always be delivered, on demand, in redemption of the paper; and also in having this paper issued by the persons who actually own the property represented by it, and who can be compelled by law to deliver it in redemption of the paper. And the great secret — if it be a secret — of having only a scanty currency, and of *not* having specie payments, consists in having the paper issued by a government that cannot fulfil its contracts, and has no intention of fulfilling them; and by banks that are not even required to fulfil them.

It is somewhat remarkable that after ten years experiment, we have not yet learned these apparently self-evident truths.

The palpable fact is that the advocates of the present "National" currency system, — that is, the stockholders in the present "National" banks, — *do not wish for specie payments.* They wish only to maintain, in their own hands, a monopoly of banking, and, as far as possible also, a monopoly of all business depending upon bank loans. They wish, therefore, to keep the volume of the currency down to its present amount. As an excuse for this, they profess a great desire for specie payments; and at the same time practice the imposture of declaring that specie payments will be impossible, if the amount of the currency be increased.

But all this is sheer falsehood and fraud. It is, of course, impossible to have specie payments, so long as the only currency issued is issued by a government that has nothing to redeem with, and has no intention of redeeming; and by banks that are not even required to redeem. But there is no obstacle to our having twenty times as much currency as we now have, and yet having specie payments — or the literal fulfilment of contracts — if we will but suffer the business of banking to go into the hands of those who have property with which to redeem, and can be compelled by law to redeem.

It is with government paper, and bank paper, as it is with the paper of private persons; that is, it is worth just what can be delivered in redemption of it, and no more. We all understand that the notes of the Astors, and Stewarts, and Vanderbilts, though issued by millions, and tens of millions, are really worth their nominal values. And why? Solely because the makers of them have the property with which to redeem them in full, and can be made to redeem them in full. We also all understand that the notes of Sam Jones, and Jim Smith, and Bill Nokes, though issued for only five dollars, are not worth two cents on the dollar. And why? Solely because they have nothing to pay with; and cannot be made to pay.

Suppose, now, that these notes of Sam Jones, and Jim Smith, and Bill Nokes, for five dollars, were the only currency allowed by law; and that they were worth in the market but two cents on the dollar. And suppose that the few holders of these notes, wishing to make the most of them, at the expense of the rights of everybody else, should keep up a constant howl for specie payments; and should protest against any issue of the notes of the Astors, the Stewarts, and the Vanderbilts, upon the ground that such issue would inflate the currency, and postpone specie payments! What would we think of men capable of uttering such absurdities ? Would we in charity to their weakness, call them idiots ? or would we in justice to their villainy, denounce them as impostors and cheats of the most transcendent and amazing impudence ? And what would we think of the wits of forty millions of people, who could be duped by such preposterous falsehoods ?

And yet this is scarcely an exaggerated picture of the fraud that has been practiced upon the people for the last ten years. A few men have secured to them-selves the monopoly of a few irredeemable notes; and not wishing to have any competition, either in the business of banking, or in any business depending upon bank loans, they cry out for specie payments; and declare that no *solvent* or *redeemable* notes must be put into circulation, in competition with their *insolvent* and *irredeemable* ones, lest the currency be inflated, and specie payments be postponed !

And this imposture is likely to be palmed off upon the people in the future, as it has been in the past, if they are such dunces as to permit it to be done.

It is perfectly evident, then, that specie payments — or the literal fulfilment of contracts — does not de-pend at all upon the amount of paper in circulation as currency ; but solely upon the fact whether, on the one hand, it be issued by those who have property with which to redeem it, and can be made to redeem it ; or whether, on the other hand, it be issued by those who cannot redeem it, and cannot be made to redeem it.

When the people shall understand these simple, man-ifest truths, they will soon put an end to the monopoly, extortion, fraud, and tyranny of the existing "National" system.

The "National" system, so called, is, in reality, no national system at all; except in the mere facts that it is called the national system, and was established by the national government. It is, in truth, only a private system; a mere privilege conferred upon a few, to enable them to control prices, property, and labor; and thus to swindle, plunder, and oppress all the rest of the people.

CHAPTER III.

NO INFLATION OF PRICES.

SECTION 1.

In reality there is no such thing as an inflation of prices, relatively to gold. There is such a thing as a depreciated paper currency. That is to say, there is such a thing as a paper currency, that is called by the same names as gold — to wit, money, dollars, &c.— but that cannot be redeemed in full; and therefore has not the same value as gold. Such a currency does not circulate at its nominal, but only at its real, value. And when such a currency is in circulation, and prices are measured by it, instead of gold, they are said to be inflated, relatively to gold. But, in reality, the prices of property are not thereby inflated at all relatively to gold. It is only the measuring of prices by a currency, that is called by the same names as gold, but that is really inferior in value to gold, that causes the *apparent*, not *real*, inflation of prices, relatively to gold.

To measure prices by a currency that is called by the same names as gold, but that is really inferior in value to gold, and then — because those prices are nominally higher than gold prices — to say that they are inflated, relatively to gold, is a perfect absurdity.

3

If we were to call a foot measure a yard, and were then to say that all cloth measured by it became thereby stretched to three times its length, relatively to a true yard-stick, we should simply make ourselves ridiculous. We should not thereby prove that the foot measure had really stretched the cloth, but only that it had taxed our brains beyond their capacity.

It is only irredeemable paper — irredeemable in whole or in part, — that ever *appears* to inflate prices, relatively to gold. But that it really causes no inflation of prices, relatively to gold, is proved by the fact that it no more inflates the prices of other property, than it does the price of gold itself. Thus we say that irredeemable paper, that is worth but fifty cents on the dollar, inflates the prices of commodities in general to twice their real value. By this we mean, that they are inflated to twice their value relatively to gold. And why do we say this? Solely because it takes twice as many of these irredeemable paper dollars to buy any commodity, — a barrel of flour for example, — as it would if the paper were equal in value to gold. But it also takes twice as many of these irredeemable paper dollars to buy gold itself, as it would if the paper were equal in value to gold. There is, therefore, just as much reason for saying that the paper inflates the price of gold, as there is for saying that it inflates the price of flour. It inflates neither. It is, itself, worth but fifty cents on the dollar; and it, therefore, takes twice as much of it to buy either flour or gold, as it would if the paper were of equal value with gold.

The value of the coins — in any nation that is open to free commerce with the rest of the world — is fixed by their value in the markets of the world; and can neither be reduced below that value, in that nation, by any possible amount of paper currency, nor raised above that value, by the entire disuse of a paper currency. Any increase of the currency, therefore, by means of paper representing other property than the coins — but having an equal value with the coins — is an absolute *bona fide* increase of the currency to that extent; and not a mere depreciation of it, as so many are in the habit of asserting.

Practically and commercially speaking, a dollar is not necessarily a specific thing, made of silver, or gold, or any other single metal, or substance. *It is only such a quantum of market value as exists in a given piece of silver or gold.* And it is the same quantum of value, whether it exist in gold, silver, houses, lands, cattle, horses, wool, cotton, wheat, iron, coal, or any other commodity that men desire for use, and buy and sell in the market.

Every dollar's worth of vendible property in the world is equal in value to a dollar in gold. And if it were possible that every dollar's worth of such property, in the world, could be represented, in the market, by a contract on paper, promising to deliver it on demand; and if every dollar's worth could be delivered on demand, in redemption of the paper that represented it, the world could then have an amount of currency equal to the entire property of the world. And yet clearly every dollar of paper would be equal in value to a dollar of gold; specie payments — or the literal fulfilment of contracts — could forever be maintained; and yet there could be no inflation of prices, relatively to gold. Such a currency would no more inflate the price of one thing, than of another. It would as much inflate the price of gold, as of any thing else. Gold would stand at its true and natural value as a metal; and all other things would also stand at their true and natural values, for their respective uses.

On this principle, if every dollar's worth of vendible property in the United States could be represented by a paper currency ; and if the property could all be delivered on demand, in redemption of the paper, such a currency would not inflate the prices of property at all, relatively to gold. Gold would still stand at its true and natural value as a metal, or at its value in the markets of the world. And all the property represented by the paper, would simply be measured by the gold, and would stand at its true and natural value, relatively to the gold.

We could then have some thirty thousand millions ($30,000,000,) of paper currency, — taking our property at its present valuation. And yet every dollar of it would be equal to a dollar of gold ; and there could evidently be no inflation of prices, relatively to gold. No more of the currency could be kept in circulation, than should be necessary or convenient for the purchase and sale of property at specie prices.

It is probably not practicable to represent the entire property of the country by such contracts on paper as would be convenient and acceptable as a currency. This is especially true of the *personal* property; although large portions even of this are being constantly represented by such contracts as bank notes, private promissory notes, checks, drafts, and bills of exchange ; all of which are in the nature of currency ; that is, they serve for the time as a substitute for specie ; although some of them do not acquire any extensive, or even general, circulation.

But that it is perfectly practicable to represent nearly all the *real estate* of the country — including the railroads — by such contracts on paper as will be perfectly convenient and acceptable as a currency ; and that every dollar of it can be kept always at par with specie throughout the entire country — that all this is perfectly practicable, the author offers the system already presented in proof.

Section 2.

To sustain their theory, that an abundant paper currency — though equal in value to gold — inflates prices, relatively to gold, its advocates assert that, *for the time being,* the paper depreciates the gold itself below its true value; or at least below that value which it had before the paper was introduced. But this is an impossibility; for in a country open to free commerce with the rest of the world, gold must always have the same value that it has in the markets of the world; neither more, nor less. No possible amount of paper can reduce it below that value; as has been abundantly demonstrated in this country for the last ten years. Neither can any possible amount of paper currency reduce gold below its only true and natural value, viz.: its value as a metal, for uses in the arts. The paper cannot reduce the gold below this value, because the paper does not come at all in competition with it for those uses. We cannot make a watch, a spoon, or a necklace, out of the paper; and therefore the paper cannot compete with the gold for these uses.

That gold and silver now have, and can be made to have, no higher value, as a currency, than they have as metals for uses in the arts, is proved by the fact that doubtless not more than one tenth, and very likely not more than a twentieth, of all the gold and silver in the world (out of the mines), is in circulation as currency. In Asia, where these metals have been accumulating from time immemorial, and whither all the gold and silver of Europe and America — except what is caught up, and converted into plate, jewelry, &c.— is now going, and has been going for the last two thousand years, very little is in circulation as money. For the common traffic of the people, coins made of coarser metals, shells, and other things of little value, are the only currency. It is only for the larger commercial transactions, that gold and silver are used at all as a currency. The great bulk of these metals are used for plate, jewelry, for embellishing temples and palaces. Large amounts are also hoarded.

But that gold and silver coins now stand, and that they can be made to stand, as currency, only at their true and natural values as metals, for uses in the arts; and that neither the use, nor disuse, of any possible amount of paper currency, in any one country — the United States, for example — can sensibly affect their values in that country, or raise them above, or reduce them below, their values in the markets of the world, the author hopes to demonstrate more fully at a future time, if it should be necessary to do so.

SECTION 3.

Another argument — or rather assertion — of those who say that any increase of the currency, by means of paper — though the paper be equal in value to gold — depreciates the value of the gold, or inflates prices relatively to gold, is this : They assert that, where no other circumstances intervene to affect the prices of particular commodities, such increase of the currency raises the prices of *all* kinds of property — relatively to gold — in a degree precisely corresponding with the increase of the currency.

This is the universal assertion of those who oppose a *solvent* paper currency; or a paper currency that is equal in value to gold.

But the assertion itself is wholly *untrue.* It is wholly *untrue* that an abundant paper currency — that is equal in value to gold — raises the prices of *all* commodities — relatively to gold — in a proportion corresponding to the increase of the currency. *Instead of doing so, it causes a rise only in agricultural commodities, and real estate; while it causes a great fall in the prices of manufactures generally.*

Thus the increased currency produces *a directly opposite effect* upon the prices of agricultural commodities and real estate, on the one hand, and upon manufactures, on the other.

The reasons are these:

Agriculture requires but very few exchanges, and can, therefore, be carried on with very little money. Manufactures, on the other hand, require a great many exchanges, and can, therefore, be carried on (except in a very feeble way), only by the aid of a great deal of money.

The consequence is, that the people of all those nations, that have but little money, are engaged mostly in agriculture. Very few of them are manufacturers. Being mostly engaged in agriculture, each one producing the same commodities with nearly all the others; and each one producing all he wants for his own consumption, there is no market, or very little market, for agricultural commodities; and such commodities, consequently, bear only a very small price.

Manufactured commodities, on the other hand, are very scarce and dear, for the sole reason that so few persons are engaged in producing them.

But let there be an increase of currency, and laborers at once leave agriculture, and become manufacturers.

As manufactured commodities usually bring much higher prices than agricultural, in proportion to the labor it costs to produce them, men usually leave agriculture, and go into manufacturing, to the full extent the increased currency will allow.

The consequence is that, under an abundant currency, manufactures become various, abundant, and cheap ; where before they were scarce and dear.

But while, on the one hand, manufactures are thus becoming various, abundant, and cheap, agricultural commodities, on the other hand, are rising : and why ? Not because the currency is depreciated, but simply because so many persons, who before — under a scanty currency — were engaged in agriculture, and produced all the agricultural commodities they needed, and perhaps more than they needed, for their own consumption, having now left agriculture, and become manufacturers, have become purchasers and consumers, instead of producers, of agricultural commodities.

Here the same cause — abundant currency — that has occasioned a *rise* in the prices of agricultural commodities, has produced a *directly opposite effect* upon manufactures. It has made the latter various, abundant, and cheap ; where before they were scarce and dear.

On the other hand, when the currency contracts, manufacturing industry is in a great degree stopped ; and the persons engaged in it are driven to agriculture as their only means of sustaining life. The consequence is, that manufactured commodities become scarce and dear, from non-production. At the same time, agricultural commodities become superabundant and cheap, from over-production and want of a market.

Thus an abundant currency, and a scanty currency, produce directly opposite effects upon the prices of

4

agricultural commodities, on the one hand, and manufactures, on the other.

The *abundant* currency makes manufactures various, abundant, and cheap, from increased production ; while it raises the prices of agricultural commodities, by withdrawing laborers from the production of them, and also by creating a body of purchasers and consumers, to wit, the manufacturers.

On the other hand, a *scanty* currency drives men from manufactures into agriculture, and thus causes manufactures to become scarce and dear, from non-production; and, at the same time, causes agricultural commodities to fall in price, from over-production, and want of a market.

But whether, on the one hand, agricultural commodities are rising, and manufactured commodities are falling, under an abundant currency; or whether, on the other hand, manufactured commodities are rising, and agricultural commodities are falling, under a scanty currency, the value of the currency itself, dollar for dollar, remains the same in both cases.

The value of the currency, in either of these cases, is fixed, not at all by the amount in circulation, but by its value relatively to gold. And the value of gold, in any particular country, is fixed by its value as a metal, and its value in the markets of the world ; and not at all by any greater or less quantity of paper that may be in circulation in that country.

SECTION 4.

But it is not alone agricultural *products* that rise in price under an abundant currency. Real estate also, of all kinds — agricultural, manufacturing, and commercial — rises under an abundant currency, and falls under a scanty currency. The reasons are these :

Agricultural real estate rises under an abundant currency, because agricultural products rise under such a currency, as already explained. *Manufacturing* real estate rises under an abundant currency, simply because — money being the great instrumentality of manufacturing industry — that industry is active and profitable under an abundant currency. *Commercial* real estate rises under an abundant currency, because, under such a currency, commerce, the exchange and distribution of agricultural and manufactured commodities, is active and profitable. *Railroads*, also, rise under an abundant currency, because, under such a currency, the transportation of freight and passengers is increased.

On the other hand, all kinds of real estate fall in price under a scanty currency, for these reasons, to wit: Agricultural real estate falls, because, manufactures having been in a great measure stopped, and the manufacturers driven into agriculture, there is little market for agricultural products, and those products bring only a small price. Manufacturing real estate falls, because, manufacturing industry having become impossible for lack of money, manufacturing real estate is lying dead, or unproductive. Commercial real estate falls, because commerce, the exchange and distribution of agricultural and manufactured commodities, has ceased. Railroads fall in price, because, owing to the suspension of manufactures and commerce, there is little transportation of either freight or passengers.

Thus it will be seen that an abundant currency creates a great rise in agricultural products, and in all kinds of real estate — agricultural, manufacturing, and commercial, (including railroads); and, at the same time, causes manufactured commodities to become various, abundant, and cheap. While, on the other hand, a scanty currency causes agricultural commodities, and all kinds of real estate, to fall in price; and, at the same time, makes manufactured commodities scarce and dear.

It is a particularly noticeable fact, that those who claim that an abundant paper currency inflates the prices of *all* commodities, relatively to gold, never find it convenient to speak of the variety, abundance, and cheapness of manufactures, that exist under an abundant currency; but only of the high prices of agricultural commodities, and real estate.

The whole subject of prices — a subject that is very little understood, and that has been forever misrepresented, in order to justify restraints upon the currency, and keep it in a few hands — deserves a more extensive discussion; but the special purposes of this pamphlet do not admit of it here. But enough has probably now been said, to show that the great changes that take place in prices, under an abundant currency, on the one hand, and a scanty currency, on the other, are not occasioned at all by any change in the value of the currency itself — dollar for dollar — provided the currency be equal in value to coin.

Enough, also, it is hoped, has been said, to show to all holders of either agricultural, manufacturing, or commercial real estate (including railroads), that the greater or less value of their property depends almost wholly upon the abundance or scarcity of currency; and that, inasmuch as, under the system proposed, they have the power, in their own hands, of creating probably all the currency that can possibly be used in manufactures and commerce, they have no one but themselves to blame, if they suffer the value of their property to be destroyed by any such narrow and tyrannical systems of currency and credit as those that now prevail, or those that have always heretofore prevailed.

By using their real estate as banking capital, they can not only get an income from it, in the shape of interest on money, but by supplying capital to mechanics and merchants, they create a large class who will pay high prices for agricultural products, and high prices and rents for manufacturing and commercial real estate ; and who will also supply them, in return, with manufactured commodities of the greatest variety, abundance, and cheapness.

It is, therefore, mere suicide for the holders of real estate, who have the power of supplying an indefinite amount of capital for mechanics and merchants — and who can make themselves and everybody else rich by supplying it — to suffer that power to be usurped by any such small body of men as those who now monopolize it, through mere favoritism, corruption, and tyranny, on the part of the government, and not because they have any claim to it.

CHAPTER IV.

Supposing the property mortgaged to be ample, the system, as a system, is absolutely secure. The currency would be absolutely incapable of insolvency; for there could never be a dollar of the currency in circulation, without a dollar of capital (Productive Stock) in bank, which *must* be transferred in redemption of it, unless redemption be made in specie.

The capital *alone*, be it observed — independently of the notes discounted — must always be sufficient to redeem the entire circulation; for the circulation can never exceed the capital (Productive Stock). But the notes discounted are also holden by the trustees, and the proceeds of them must be applied to the redemption of the circulation. Supposing, therefore, the capital to be sufficient, and the notes discounted to be solvent, the redemption of the circulation is doubly secured.

What guarantee, then, have the public, for the sufficiency of the mortgages? They have these, viz.:

1. The mortgages, composing the capital of a bank, will be matters of public record, and everybody, *in the neighborhood*, will have the means of judging for himself of the sufficiency of the property holden. If the

property should be insufficient, the bank would be discredited at once ; for the abundance of solvent currency would be so great, that no one would have any inducement to take that which was insolvent or doubtful.

2. By the Articles of Association, all the mortgages that make up the capital of a bank, are made mutually responsible for each other; because, if any one mortgage proves insufficient, no dividend can afterwards be paid to any of the bankers (mortgagors), until that deficiency shall have been made good by the company· The effect of this provision will be, to make all the founders of a bank look carefully to the sufficiency of each other's mortgages; because no man will be willing to put in a good mortgage of his own, on equal terms with a bad mortgage of another man's, when he knows that his own mortgage will have to contribute to making good any deficiency of the other. The result will be, that the mortgages, that go to make up the capital of any one bank, *will be either all good, or all bad*. If they are *all good*, the solvency of the bank will be apparent to all *in the vicinity ;* and the credit of the bank will at once be established *at home.* If the mortgages are *all bad*, that fact, also, will be apparent to everybody *in the vicinity*, and the bank is at once discredited *at home.*

From the foregoing considerations, it is evident that nothing is easier than for a *good* bank to establish its credit, *at home ;* and that nothing is more certain than that a *bad* bank would be discredited, *at home*, from the outset, and could get no circulation at all.

37

It is also evident that a bank, that has no credit at home, could get none abroad. There is, therefore, no danger of the public being swindled by bad banks.

A bank that is well founded, and that has established its credit at home, has so many ways of establishing its credit abroad, that there is no need that they be all specified here. The mode that seems most likely to be adopted, is the following, viz. :

When the capital shall consist of mortgages, it will be very easy for all the banks, in any one State, to make their solvency known to each other. There would be so many banks, that some system would naturally be adopted for this purpose.

Perhaps this system would be, that a standing committee, appointed by the banks, would be established in each State, to whom each bank in the State would be required to produce satisfactory evidence of its solvency, before its bills should be received by the other banks of the State.

When the banks, or any considerable number of the banks, of any particular State — Massachusetts, for instance, — shall have made themselves so far acquainted with each other's solvency, as to be ready to receive each other's bills, they will be ready to make a still further arrangement for their mutual benefit, viz: To unite in establishing one general agency in Boston, another in New York, and others in Philadelphia, Baltimore, Cincinnati, Chicago, St. Louis, New Orleans, San Francisco, &c., &c., where the bills of all these Massachusetts banks would be redeemed, either

5

from a common fund contributed for the purpose, or in such other way as might be found best. And thus the bills of all the Massachusetts banks would be placed at par at all the great commercial points.

Each bank, belonging to the association, might print on the back of its bills, "*Redeemable at the Massachusetts Agencies in Boston, New York, Philadelphia, &c.*"

In this way, all the banks of each State might unite to establish a joint agency in every large city, throughout the country, for the redemption of all their bills. In doing so, they would not only certify, but make themselves responsible for, the solvency of each other's bills.

The banks might safely make *permanent* arrangements of this kind with each other; because the *permanent* solvency of all the banks might be relied on.

The permanent solvency of all the banks might be relied on, because, under this system, a bank (whose capital consists of mortgages), once solvent, is necessarily forever solvent, unless in contingencies so utterly improbable as not to need to be taken into account. In fact, in the ordinary course of things, every bank would be growing more and more solvent; because, in the ordinary course of things, the mortgaged property would be constantly rising in value, as the wealth and population of the country should increase. The exceptions to this rule would be so rare as to be unworthy of notice.

There is, therefore, no difficulty in putting the currency, furnished by each State, at par throughout the United States.

At the general agencies, in the great cities, the redemption would, doubtless, *so far as necessary*, be made in specie, *on demand;* because, at such points, especially in cities on the sea-board, there would always be an abundance of specie in the market as merchandise ; and it would, therefore, be both for the convenience and interest of the banks to redeem in specie, on demand, rather than transfer a portion of their capital, and then pay interest on that capital until it should be redeemed, or bought back, with specie.

Often, however, and very likely even in the great majority of cases, a man from one State — as California, for example, — presenting Massachusetts bills for redemption at a Massachusetts agency — either in Boston, New York, or elsewhere — would prefer to have them redeemed with bills from his own State, California, rather than with specie.

If the system were adopted throughout the United States, the banks of each State would be likely to have agencies of this kind in all the great cities. Each of these agencies would exchange the bills of every other State for the bills of its own State ; and thus the bills of each State would find their way home, without any demand for their redemption in specie having ever been made.

Where railroads were used as capital, all the banks in the United States could form one association, of the kind just mentioned, to establish agencies at all the great commercial points, for the redemption of their bills.

Of course each railroad would receive the bills of all other roads, for fare and freight.

Thus all railroad currency, under this system, would be put at par throughout the United States.

CHAPTER V.

THE SYSTEM AS A CREDIT SYSTEM.

SECTION 1.

Perhaps the merits of the system, as a credit system, cannot be better illustrated than by comparing the amount of loanable capital it is capable of supplying, with the amount which the present "National" banks (so called) are capable of supplying.

If we thus compare the two systems, we shall find that the former is capable of supplying more than fifty times as much credit as the latter.

Thus the entire circulation authorized by all the "National" banks,* is but three hundred and fifty-four millions of dollars ($354,000,000).

But the real estate and railroads of the country are probably worth twenty thousand millions of dollars ($20,000,000,000). This latter sum is fifty-six times greater than the former; and is all capable of being loaned in the form of currency.

Calling the population of the country forty millions (40,000,000), the "National" system is capable of supplying not quite *nine* dollars ($9) of loanable cap-

---

* Exclusive of the so-called "gold" banks, which are too few to be worthy of notice.

ital to each individual of the whole population. The system proposed is capable of supplying five hundred dollars ($500) of loanable capital to each individual of the whole population.

Supposing one half the population (male and female) to be sixteen years of age and upwards, and to be capable of producing wealth, and to need capital for their industry, the "National" system would furnish not quite eighteen dollars ($18) for each one of them, on an average. The other system is capable of furnishing one thousand dollars $1,000) for each one of them, on an average.

Supposing the adults (both male and female) of the country to be sixteen millions (16,000,000), the "National" system is capable of furnishing only twenty-two dollars and twelve and a half cents ($22.12½) to each one of these persons, on an average. The system proposed is capable of furnishing twelve hundred and fifty dollars ($1,250) to each one, on an average.

Supposing the number of *male* adults in the whole country to be eight millions (8,000,000), the "National" system is capable of furnishing only forty-four dollars and twenty-five cents ($44.25) to each one. The other system is capable of furnishing twenty-five hundred dollars ($2,500) to each one.

The present number of "National" banks is little less than two thousand (2,000). Calling the number two thousand (2,000), and supposing the $354,000,000 of circulation to be equally divided between them, each bank would be authorized to issue $177,000.

Under the proposed system, the real estate and railroads of the country are capable of furnishing one hundred thousand (100,000) banks, having each a capital of two hundred thousand dollars ($200,000); or it is capable of furnishing one hundred and twelve thousand nine hundred and ninety-four (112,994) banks, having each a capital ($177,000), equal, on an average, to the capital of the present "National" banks. That is, this system is capable of furnishing fifty-six times as many banks as the "National" system, having each the same capital, on an average, as the "National" banks.

Calling the number of the present "National" banks two thousand (2,000), and the population of the country forty millions (40,000,000), there is only one bank to 20,000 people, on an average; each bank being authorized to issue, on an average, a circulation of $177,000.

Under the proposed system, we could have one bank for every five hundred (500) persons; each bank being authorized to issue $200,000; or $23,000 each more than the "National" banks.

These figures give some idea of the comparative capacity of the two systems to furnish credit.

Under which of these two systems, now, would everybody, who needs credit, and deserves it, be most likely to get it? And to get all he needs to make his industry most productive? And to get it at the lowest rates of interest?

The proposed system is as much superior to the old specie paying system (so called) — in respect to the

amount of loanable capital it is capable of supplying—
as it is to the present "National" system.

Section 2.

But the proposed system has one other feature,
which is likely to be of great practical importance, and
which gives it a still further superiority — as a credit
system — over the so-called specie paying system. It
is this:

The old specie paying system (so called) could add
to the loanable capital of the country, *only by so much
currency as it could keep in circulation, over and above
the amount of specie that it was necessary to keep on
hand for its redemption.* But the amount of loanable
capital which the proposed system can supply, hardly
depends at all upon the amount of its currency that
can be kept in circulation. It can supply about the
same amount of loanable capital, even though its currency should be returned for redemption immediately
after it is issued. It can do this, because the banks,
*by paying interest on the currency returned for redemp-
tion* — or, what is the same thing, by paying dividends
on the Productive Stock transferred in redemption of
the currency — can postpone the payment of specie to
such time as it shall be convenient for them to pay it.

All that would be necessary to make loans practicable on this basis, would be, that the banks should
receive a higher rate of interest on their loans than
they would have to pay on the currency returned for

redemption; that is, on the PRODUCTIVE STOCK transferred in redemption of the currency.

The rate of interest *received* by the banks, on the
loans made by them, would need to be so much higher
than that *paid* by them, on currency returned for
redemption, as to make it an object for them to loan
more of their currency than could be kept in circulation. Subject to this condition, the banks could loan
their entire capitals, whether much or little of it could
be kept in circulation.

For example, suppose the banks should pay *six* per
cent. interest on currency returned for redemption —
(or as dividends on the PRODUCTIVE STOCK transferred
in redemption of such currency) — they could then
loan their currency at *nine* per cent. and still make
three per cent. profits, even though the currency loaned
should come back for redemption immediately after it
was issued.

But this is not all. Even though the banks should
pay, on currency returned for redemption, precisely
the same rate of interest they *received* on loans — say
six per cent. — they could still do business, if their
currency should, on an average, continue in circulation
one half the time for which it was loaned; for then the
banks would get three per cent. net on their loans, and
this would make their business a paying one.

But the banks would probably do much better than
this; for bank credits would supersede all private
credits; and the diversity and amount of production
would be so great that an immense amount of currency

6

would be constantly required to make the necessary exchanges. And whatever amount should be necessary for making these exchanges, would, of course, remain in circulation. However much currency, therefore, should be issued, it is probable that, on an average, it would remain in circulation more than half the time for which it was loaned.

Or if the banks should pay *six* per cent. interest on currency returned for redemption; and should then loan money, for *six* months, at *eight* per cent. interest; and this currency should remain in circulation but one month; the banks would then get eight per cent. for the one month, and two per cent. net for the other five months; which would be equal to three per cent. for the whole six months. Or ·if the currency should remain in circulation two months, the banks would then get eight per cent. for the two months, and two per cent. net for the other four months; which would be equal to four per cent. for the whole six months. Or if the currency should remain in circulation three months, the banks would then get eight per cent. for three months, and two per cent. net for the other three months; which would be equal to five per cent. for the whole six months. Or if the currency should remain in circulation four months, the banks would then get eight per cent. for the four months, and two per cent. net for the other two months; which would be equal to six per cent. for the whole six months. Or if the currency should remain in circulation five months, the banks would then get eight per cent. for the five months, and two per cent. net for the other month; which would be equal to seven per cent. for the whole six months.

The banks would soon ascertain, by experiment, how long their currency was likely to remain in circulation; and what rate of interest it was therefore necessary for them to charge to make their business a paying one. And that rate, whatever it might be, the borrowers would have to pay. Subject to this condition, the banks could always loan their entire capitals.

CHAPTER VI.

AMOUNT OF CURRENCY NEEDED.

It is of no use to say that we do not need so much currency as the proposed system would supply; because, first, if we should not need it, we shall not use it. Every dollar of paper will represent specific property that can be delivered on demand in redemption of it, and that will have the same market value as gold. The paper dollar, therefore, will have the same market value as the gold dollar, or as a dollar's worth of any other property; and no one will part with it, unless he gets in exchange for it something that will serve his particular wants better; and no one will accept it, unless it will serve his particular wants better than the thing he parts with. No more paper, therefore, can circulate, than is wanted for the purchase and sale of commodities at their true and natural values, as measured by gold.

Secondly, we do not know at all how much currency we do need. That is something that can be determined only by experiment. We know that, heretofore, whenever currency has been increased, industry and traffic have increased to a corresponding extent. And they would unquestionably increase to an extent far beyond any thing the world has ever seen, if only they were aided and permitted by an adequate currency.

We, as yet, know very little what wealth mankind are capable of creating. It is only within a hundred years, or a little more, that any considerable portion of them have really begun to invent machinery, and learned that it is only by machinery that they can create any considerable wealth. But they have not yet learned—at least, they profess not to have learned—that money is indispensable to the practical employment of machinery ; that it is as impossible to operate machinery without money, as it is to operate it without wind, water, or steam. When they shall have learned, and practically accepted, this great fact, and shall have provided themselves with money, wealth will speedily become universal. And it is only those who would deplore such a result, or those who are too stupid to see the palpable and necessary connection between money and manufacturing industry, who resist the indefinite increase of money.

It is scarcely a more patent fact that land is the indispensable capital for agricultural industry, than it is that money is the indispensable capital for manufacturing industry. Practically, everybody recognizes this fact, and virtually acknowledges it ; although, in words, so many deny it. Men as deliberately and accurately calculate the amount of machinery that a hundred dollars in money will operate, as they do the amount of machinery that a ton of coal, or a given amount of water, will operate. They calculate much more accurately the amount of manufactured goods a hundred dollars will produce, than they do the amount of grain, grass, or vegetables an acre of land will produce. They no more expect to see mechanics carrying on business for themselves without money, than they do to see agricultural laborers carrying on farming without land, or than they do to see sailors going to sea without ships. They know that all mechanical, as well as agricultural, laborers, who have not the appropriate capital for their special business, must necessarily stand idle, or become mere wage-laborers for others, at such particular employments as the latter may dictate, and at such prices as the latter may see fit to pay.

All these things attest the perfect knowledge that men have, that a money capital is indispensable to manufacturing industry; whatever assertions they may make to the contrary.

They know, therefore, that prohibitions upon money are prohibitions upon industry itself; that there can be no such thing as freedom of industry, where there is not freedom to lend and hire capital for such industry.

Every one knows, too — who knows any thing at all on such a subject — that it is, intrinsically, as flagrant a tyranny, as flagrant a violation of men's natural rights, for a government to forbid the lending and hiring of money for manufacturing industry, as it is to forbid the lending and hiring of land, or agricultural implements, for agricultural industry, or the lending and hiring of ships for maritime industry. They know that it is as flagrant a tyranny, as flagrant a violation of men's natural rights, to forbid one man to lend another money for mechanical industry, as it would be to forbid the former to lend the latter a house to live in, a shop to work in, or tools to work with.

It is, therefore, a flagrant, manifest tyranny, a flagrant, manifest violation of men's natural rights, to lay any conditions or restrictions whatever upon the business of banking — that is, upon the lending and hiring of money — except such as are laid upon all other transactions between man and man, viz. : the fulfilment of contracts, and restraints upon force and fraud.

A man who is without capital, and who, by prohibitions upon banking, is practically forbidden to hire any, is in a condition elevated but one degree above that of a chattel slave. He may live ; but he can live only as the servant of others ; compelled to perform such labor, and to perform it at such prices, as they may see fit to dictate. And a government, which, at this day, subjects the great body of the people — or even any portion of them — to this condition, is as fit an object of popular retribution as any tyranny that ever existed.

To deprive mankind of their natural right and power of creating wealth for themselves, is as great a tyranny as it is to rob them of it after they have created it. And this is done by all laws against honest banking.

All these things are so self-evident, so universally known, that no man, of ordinary mental capacity, can claim to be ignorant of them. And any legislator, who disregards them, should be taught, by a discipline short, sharp, and decisive, that his power is wholly subordinate to the natural rights of mankind.

It is, then, one of man's indisputable, natural rights to lend and hire capital in any and every form and manner that is intrinsically honest. And as money, or currency, is the great, the indispensable instrumentality in the production and distribution of wealth; as it is the capital, the motive power, that sets all other instrumentalities in motion; as it is the one thing, without . which all the other great agencies of production — such as science, skill, and machinery — are practically paralyzed; to say that we need no more of it, and shall have no more of it, than we now have, is to say that we need no more wealth, and shall have no more wealth, and no more equal or equitable distribution of wealth, than we now have. It is to say that the mass of mankind — the laborers, the producers of wealth — need not to produce, and shall not be permitted to produce, wealth for themselves, but only for others.

For a government to limit the currency of a people, and to designate the individuals (or corporations) who shall have the control of that currency, is, manifestly, equivalent to saying there shall be but so much industry and wealth in the nation, and that these shall be under the special control, and for the special enjoyment, of the individuals designated; and, of course, that all other persons shall be simply their dependants and servants; receiving only such prices for their property, and such compensation for their labor, as these few holders of the currency shall see fit to give for them.

The effect of these prohibitions upon money, and consequently upon industry, are everywhere apparent in the poverty of the great body of the people.

At the present time, the people of this country certainly do not produce one third, very likely not one fifth, of the wealth they might produce. And the little they do produce is all in the hands of a few. All this is attributable to the want of currency and credit, and to the consequent want of science, skill, machinery, and working capital.

Of the twenty million persons, male and female, of sixteen years of age and upwards — capable of producing wealth — certainly not one in five has the science, skill, implements, machinery, and capital necessary to make his or her industry most effective ; or to secure to himself or herself the greatest share in the products of his or her own industry. A very large proportion of these persons — nearly all the females, and a great majority of the males — persons capable of running machinery, and of producing each three, five, or ten dollars of wealth per day, are now without science, skill, machinery, or capital, and are either producing nothing, or working only with such inferior means, and at such inferior employments, as to make their industry of scarcely any value at all, either to themselves or others, beyond the provision of the coarsest necessaries of a hard and coarse existence.

7

And this is all owing to the lack of money; or rather to the lack of money and credit.

There are, doubtless, in the country, ten million (10,000,000) persons, male and female — sixteen years of age and upwards — who are naturally capable of creating from three to five dollars of wealth per day, if they had the science, skill, machinery, and capital which they ought to have, and might have; but who, from the want of these, are now creating not more than one dollar each per day, on an average; thus occasioning a loss to themselves and the country of from twenty to forty millions of dollars per day, for three hundred days in a year; a sum equal to from six to twelve thousand millions per annum; or three to six times the amount of our entire national debt.

And there are another ten million of persons — better supplied, indeed, with capital, machinery, &c., than the ten million before mentioned — but who, nevertheless, from the same causes, are producing far less than they might.

The aggregate loss to the country, from these causes, is, doubtless, equal to from ten to fifteen thousand millions per year; or five, six, or seven times the amount of the entire national debt.

In this estimate no account is taken of the loss suffered from our inability — owing simply to a want of money — to bring to this country, and give employment to, the millions of laborers, in Europe and Asia, who desire to come here, and add the products of their labor to our national wealth.

It is, probably, no more than a reasonable estimate to suppose that the nation, as a nation, is losing twenty thousand millions of dollars ($20,000,000,000) per annum — about ten times the amount of our national debt — solely for the want of money to give such employment as they need, to the population we now have, and to those who desire to come here from other countries.

Among the losses we suffer, from the causes mentioned, the non-production of new inventions is by no means the least. As a general rule, new inventions are made only where money and machinery prevail. And they are generally produced in a ratio corresponding with the amount of money and machinery. In no part of the country are the new inventions equal in number to what they ought to be, and might be. In three fourths of the country very few are produced. In some, almost none at all. The losses from this cause cannot be estimated in money.

The government, in its ignorance, arrogance, and tyranny, either does not see all this, or, seeing it, does not regard it. While these thousands of millions are being lost annually, from the suppression of money, and consequently of industry, and while three fourths of the laborers of the country are either standing idle, or, for the want of capital, are producing only a mere fraction of what they might produce, a two-pence-ha'-penny Secretary of the Treasury can find no better employment for his faculties, than in trying, first, to reduce the rate of interest on the public debt one per cent.— thereby saving twenty millions a year, *or fifty cents for each person, on an average!* And, secondly, in paying one hundred millions per annum of the principal; that is, *two and a half dollars for each person, on an average!* And he insists that the only way to achieve these astounding results, is to deprive the people at large of money! To destroy, as far as possible, their industry! To deprive them, as far as possible, of all power to manufacture for themselves! And to compel them to pay, to the few manufacturers it has under its protection, fifty or one hundred per cent. more for their manufactures than they are worth!

He has been tugging at this tremendous task four years, or thereabouts. And he confidently believes that if he can be permitted to enforce this plan for a sufficient period of years, in the future, he will ultimately be able to save the people, annually, *fifty cents each, on an average, in interest!* and also continue to pay, annually, *two dollars and a half for each person, on an average,* of the principal, of the national debt !

He apparently does not know, or, if he knows, it is, in his eyes, a matter of comparatively small moment, that this saving of $20,000,000 per annum in interest, and this payment of $100,000,000 per annum of principal, which he proposes to make on behalf of the people, are not equal to what *two days* — or perhaps even *one day* — of their industry would amount to, if they were permitted to enjoy their natural rights of lending and hiring capital, and producing such wealth as they please for themselves.

He apparently does not know, or, if he knows, it is with him a small matter, that if the people were permitted to enjoy their natural freedom in currency and credit, and consequently their natural freedom in industry, they could pay the entire national debt three, four, or a half dozen times over *every year,* more easily than they can save the $20,000,000, and pay the $100,000,000, annually, by the process that he adopts for saving and paying them.

And yet this man, and his policy, represent the government and its policy. The president keeps him in office, and Congress sustain him in his measures.

In short, the government not only does not offer, but is apparently determined not to suffer, any such thing as freedom in currency and credit, or, consequently, in industry. It is, apparently, so bent upon compelling the people to give more for its few irredeemable notes than they are worth; and so bent upon keeping all wealth, and all means of wealth, in the hands of the few — upon whose money and frauds it relies for support — that it is determined, if possible, to perpetuate this state of things indefinitely. And it will probably succeed in perpetuating it indefinitely — under cover of such false pretences as those of specie payments, inflation of prices, reducing the interest, and paying the principal, of the national debt, &c. — unless the people at large shall open their eyes to the deceit and robbery that are practised upon them; and, by establishing freedom in currency and credit — and thereby freedom in industry and commerce — end at once and forever the tyranny that impoverishes and enslaves them.

CHAPTER VII.

IMPORTANCE OF THE SYSTEM TO MASSACHUSETTS.

Section 1.

The tariffs, by means of which a few monied men of Massachusetts have so long plundered the rest of the country, and on which they have so largely relied for their prosperity, will not much longer be endured. The nation at large has no need of tariffs. Money is the great instrumentality for manufacturing. And the nation needs nothing but an ample supply of money — in addition to its natural advantages — to enable our people to manufacture for themselves much more cheaply than any other people can manufacture for us.

To say nothing of the many millions who, if we had the money necessary to give them employment, might be brought here from Europe and Asia, and employed in manufactures, more than half the productive power of our present population — in the South and West much more than half — is utterly lost for the want of money, and the consequent want of science, skill, and machinery. And yet those few, who monopolize the present stock of money, insist that they must have tariffs to enable them to manufacture at all. And the nation is duped by these false pretences.

To give bounties to encourage manufactures, and at the same time forbid all but a favored few to have money to manufacture with, is just as absurd as it would be to give bounties to encourage manufactures, and at the same time forbid all but a favored few to have machinery of any kind to manufacture with. It is just as absurd as it would be to give bounties to encourage agriculture, and at the same time forbid all but a favored few to own land, or have cattle, horses, seed corn, seed wheat, or agricultural implements. It is just as absurd as it would be to give bounties to encourage navigation, and at the same time forbid all but a favored few to have ships.

The whole object of such absurdities and tyrannies is to commit the double wrong of depriving the mass of the people of all power to manufacture for themselves, and at the same time compel them to pay extortionate prices to the favored few who are permitted to manufacture.

When tariffs shall be abolished, Massachusetts will have no means of increasing her prosperity, nor even of perpetuating such poor prosperity as she now has,* except by a great increase of money; such an increase of money as will enable her skilled laborers and enterprising young men to get capital for such industries and enterprises as they may prefer to engage in here, rather than go elsewhere.

Even if Massachusetts were willing to manufacture

---

* I say "poor prosperity," because the present prosperity of Massachusetts is not only a dishonest prosperity, but is also only the prosperity of the few, and not of the many.

for the South and West, *without a tariff*, she could hope to do so only until the South and West should supply themselves with money. So soon as they shall supply themselves with money, they will be able to manufacture for themselves more cheaply than Massachusetts can manufacture for them. Their natural advantages for manufacturing are greatly superior to those of Massachusetts. They have the cheap food, coal, iron, lead, copper, wool, cotton, hides, &c., &c. They lack only money to avail themselves of these advantages. And, under the system proposed, their lands and railroads are capable of supplying all the money they need. And they will soon adopt that, or some other system. And they will then not only be independent of Massachusetts, but will be able to draw away from her her skilled laborers, and enterprising young men, unless she shall first supply them with the money capital necessary for such industries and enterprises as may induce them to remain. They will, of course, go where they can get capital, instead of staying where they can get none.

So great are the natural advantages of the South and West over those of Massachusetts, that it is doubtful how many of these men can be persuaded to remain, by all the inducements that capital can offer. But without such inducements it is certain they will all go.

And Massachusetts has no means of supplying this needed money, except by using her real estate as banking capital.

8

It is, therefore, plainly a matter of life or death to the holders of real estate in Massachusetts to use it for that purpose ; for their real estate will be worth nothing when the skilled labor and the enterprising young men of Massachusetts shall have deserted her.

All this is so manifest as to need no further demonstration. And Massachusetts will do well to look the facts in the face before it is too late.

SECTION 2.

What prospect has Massachusetts under the present " National " system ?

The Comptroller of the Currency, in his last annual report, says, that of the $354,000,000 of circulation authorized by law, Massachusetts has now $58,506,686. He says, further, that this is more than four times as much as she would be entitled to, if the currency were apportioned equally among the States, according to population ; more than twice as much as she would be entitled to, if the circulation were apportioned among the States, according to their wealth ; and three times as much as she is entitled to upon an apportionment made — as apportionments are now professedly made — half upon population, and half upon wealth.

The Comptroller further says, that a law of Congress, passed July 12, 1870, requiring him to withdraw circulation from those States having more than their just proportion, and to distribute it among those now having less than their just proportion, will require him to withdraw "from thirty-six banks in the City of Boston, $11,403,000; [and] from fifty-three country banks of Massachusetts, $2,997,000."

Thus the law requires $14,400,000 to be withdrawn from the present banks of Massachusetts.

When this shall have been done, she will have but $44,106,686 left. And as this will be more than three times her just proportion on a basis of population, and nearly twice her just share on a basis of wealth, there is no knowing how soon the remaining excess over her just share may be withdrawn.*

By the census of 1870, Massachusetts had a population of 1,457,351. She has now, doubtless, a population of 1,500,000. Calling her population 1,500,000, the $58,506,686 of circulation which she now has, is equal to $39 for each person, on an average. When $14,400,000 of this amount shall have been withdrawn, as the law now requires it to be, the circulation will be reduced to less than $30 for each person, on an average. If the circulation should be reduced to the proportion to which Massachusetts is entitled, on the basis of wealth — that is, to $25,098,600 — she will then have less than $17 for each person, on an average. If the circulation should be reduced to the proportion to which Massachusetts is entitled on a basis of population — that is to $13,879,778 — she will then have a trifle less than $9 for each person, on an average.

For years the industry of Massachusetts has been

---

* If the excess mentioned in the text should not be withdrawn, it will be only because the system is so villainous in itself, that other parts of the country will not accept the shares to which they are entitled.

greatly crippled for the want of bank credits, although her banks have been authorized to issue their notes to the amount of $58,506,686; or $39 to each person, on an average. What will her industry be when her banks shall be authorized to issue only $44,106,686, or $30 for each person, on an average? What will it be, if her bank issues shall be reduced to her proportion on a basis of wealth, to wit, $25,098,600; or less than $17 for each person, on an average? Or what will it be, if her bank circulation shall be reduced to her proportion on a basis of population, to wit, to $13,379,778; or less than $9 for each person, on an average?

In contrast with such contemptible sums as these, Massachusetts, under the system proposed, could have nine hundred millions ($900,000,000) of bank loans; * that is, $600 for every man, woman, and child, on an average; or $1,500 to each adult, male and female, on an average; or $3,000 to each *male* adult, on an average.

Which, now, of these two systems is most likely to secure and increase the prosperity of Massachusetts? Which is most likely to give to every deserving man and woman in the State, the capital necessary to make their industry most productive to themselves individually, and to the State? Which system is most likely to induce the skilled laborers and enterprising young men of Massachusetts to remain here? And which is most likely to drive them away?

* Since the notes on page fifth were printed, the *Boston Journal*, of Jan. 11, 1873, says that, by the valuation of 1872, the real estate of Massachusetts is $1.131,306,347.

SECTION 3.

But the whole is not yet told. The present "National" system is so burdened with taxes and other onerous conditions, that no banking at all can be done under it, except at rates of interest that are two or three times as high as they ought to be; or as they would be under the system proposed.

The burdens imposed on the present banks are probably equal to from six to eight per cent. *upon the amount of their own notes that they are permitted to issue.*

In the first place, they are required, for every $90 of circulation, to invest $100 in five or six per cent. government bonds.* This alone is a great burden to all that class of persons who want their capital for active business. It amounts to actual prohibition upon all whose property is in real estate, and therefore not convertible into bonds. And this is a purely tyrannical provision, inasmuch as real estate is a much safer and better capital than the bonds. Let us call this a burden of *two per cent. on their circulation.*

Next, is the risk as to the permanent value of the bonds. Any war, civil or foreign, would cause them to

---

* At first they were required to invest only in *six* per cent. bonds. But more recently they have been coerced or "persuaded" to invest sixty-five millions ($65,000,000) in *five* per cent. bonds. And very lately it has been announced that "The Comptroller of the Currency will not hereafter change United States bonds, deposited as security for circulating notes of national banks, except upon condition of substituting the new five per cents. of the loan of July 14, 1870, and January 20, 1872." — *Boston Daily Advertiser of February* 5, 1873.

From this it is evident that all the banks are to be "persuaded" into investing their capitals in *five* per cent. bonds.

drop in value, as the frost causes the mercury to drop in the thermometer. Even any danger of war would at once reduce them in value. Let us call this risk another burden of *one per cent. on the circulation*.

Next, every bank in seventeen or eighteen of the largest cities — Boston among the number — are required to keep on hand, at all times, a reserve — *in dead capital* (legal tenders) — " equal to at least twenty-five per centum," and all other banks a similar reserve " equal to at least fifteen per centum," " of the aggregate amount of their *notes in circulation, and of their deposits*."

Doubtless, two thirds — very likely three fourths — of all the bank circulation and deposits are in the seventeen cities named. And as these city banks are required to keep a reserve of dead capital equal to twenty-five per cent., and all others a similar reserve equal to fifteen per cent., *both on their circulation and deposits*, this average burden on all the banks is, doubtless, equal to *two per cent. on their circulation*.

Next, the banks are required to pay to the United States an annual tax of one per cent. on their average circulation, and half of one per cent. on the amount of their deposits.

Here is another burden equal to at least *one and a half per cent. on their circulation*.

Then the capitals of the banks — the United States bonds — are made liable to State taxes to any extent, " not at a greater rate than is assessed upon the monied capital in the hands of individual citizens of such

State." This tax is probably equal to *one per cent. on their circulation.*

Here, then, are taxes and burdens equal to *seven and a half per cent. on their circulation.*

Next, the banks are required to make at least *five* reports annually, to the Comptroller of the Currency, of their "resources and liabilities." Also reports of "the amount of each dividend declared by the association."

Then, too, the banks are restricted as to the rates of interest they are permitted to take.

Then "Congress may at any time alter, amend, or repeal this act;" and thus impose upon the banks still further taxes, conditions, restrictions, returns, and reports. Or it may at pleasure abolish the banks altogether.

All these taxes, burdens, and liabilities, cannot be reckoned at less than *eight or nine per cent. on the circulation of the banks;* a sum two or three times as great as the rate of interest ought to be; and two or three times as great as it would be under the system proposed.

And yet the banks must submit to all these burdens as a condition of being permitted to loan money at all. And they must make up — in their rates of interest — for all these burdens. Under this system, therefore, the rate of interest must always be two or three times as high as it ought to be.

The objections to the system, then, are, first, that it furnishes very little loanable capital; and, second, that it necessarily raises the interest on that little to two or three times what it ought to be.

Such a system, obviously, could not be endured at all, but for these reasons, viz. : first, that, being a monopoly, those holding it are enabled to make enormous extortions upon borrowers; and, secondly, that these borrowers — most of whom are the bankers themselves — employ the money in the manufacture and sale of goods that are protected, by tariffs, from foreign competition, and for which they are thus enabled to get, say, fifty per cent. more than they are worth.

In this way, these bank extortions and tariff extortions are thrown ultimately upon the people who consume the goods which the bank capital is employed in producing and selling.

Thus the joint effect of the bank system and the tariff is, first, to deprive the mass of the people of the money capital that would enable them to manufacture for themselves ; and, secondly, to compel them to pay extortionate prices for the few manufactures that are produced.

Under the system proposed, all these things would be done away. The West and the South, that are now relied on to pay all these extortions, would manufacture for themselves. Their lands and railroads would enable them to supply all the manufacturing capital that could be used. And they could supply it at one half, or one third, the rates now required by the " National " banks. Of course, Massachusetts could not —

under the "National" system — manufacture a dollar's worth for the South and West. She could not keep her manufacturing laborers. They would all go where they could get cheap capital, cheap supplies, and good markets. And then the manufacturing industry of Massachusetts, and with it the value of her real estate, will have perished from the natural and legitimate effect of her meanness, extortion, and tyranny.

Looking to the future, then, there is no State in the Union — certainly none outside of New England — that has a greater interest in supplying her mechanics with the greatest possible amount of capital; or in supplying it at the lowest possible rates of interest. And this can be done only by using her real estate as banking capital.

9

CHAPTER VIII.

THE TRUE CHARACTER OF THE "NATIONAL" SYSTEM.

SECTION 1.

Under the "National" system there are less than 2,000 banks. But let us call them 2,000.

Calling the population of the country forty millions, there is but one bank to 20,000 people.

And this one bank is, *in law*, a person; and only a single person. In lending money, it acts, and can act, only as a unit. Its several stockholders cannot act separately, as so many individuals, in lending money.

So far, therefore, as this system is concerned, *there is but one money lender for twenty thousand people!*

Of these 20,000 people, ten thousand (male and female) are sixteen years of age and upwards, capable of creating wealth, and requiring capital to make their labor most productive.

Yet, so far as this system is concerned, there is but one person authorized to lend money to, or for, these ten thousand, who wish to borrow.

And this one money lender is one who, proverbially "has no soul." It is not a natural human being. It is a legal, an artificial, and not a natural, person. It is neither masculine nor feminine. It has not the ordinary human sympathies, and is not influenced by the ordinary human motives of action. It is no father, who might wish to lend money to his children, to start them in life. It is no neighbor, who might wish to assist his neighbor. It is no citizen, who might wish to promote the public welfare. It is simply a nondescript, created by law, that wants money, and nothing else.

Moreover, it has only $177,000 to lend to these 10,000 borrowers; *that is, a fraction less than $18, on an average, for each one!*

What chance of borrowing capital have these ten thousand persons, who are forbidden to borrow, except from this one soulless person, who has so little to lend?

If money lenders must be soulless — as, perhaps, to some extent, they must be — it is certainly of the utmost importance that there be so many of them, and that they may have so much money to lend, as that they may be necessitated, by their own selfishness, to compete with each other, and thus save the borrowers from their extortions.

But the "National" system says, not only that the money lender shall be a soulless person, and one having only a little money to lend, but that he shall also have the whole field — a field of 10,000 borrowers — entirely to himself!

It says that this soulless person shall have this whole field to himself, notwithstanding he has so little money to lend, and notwithstanding there are many other persons standing by, having, in the aggregate, fifty times as much money to lend as he; and desiring to lend it at one half, or one third, the rates he is demanding, and extorting!

It says, too, that he shall have this whole field to himself, notwithstanding that ninety-nine one-hundredths of those who desire to borrow, are sent away empty! and are thereby condemned — so far as such a system can condemn them — to inevitable poverty!

Section 2.

But further. Each one of these 2,000 legal, or artificial, persons, who alone are permitted to *lend* money, is made up of, say, fifty actual, or natural, persons, to whom alone, it is well known, that this legal person will lend it!

These 2,000 legal persons, then, who alone are permitted to lend money, are made up of 100,000 actual persons, who alone are to borrow it.

These 100,000 actual persons, who compose the legal persons, do not, then, become bankers because they have money to lend to others, but only because they themselves want to borrow!

Thus when the system says that they alone shall lend, it virtually says that they alone shall borrow; because it is well known that, in practice, they *will* lend only to themselves.

In short, it says that only these 100,000 men — or one in four hundred of the population — shall have liberty either to lend, or borrow, capital! Such capital as is indispensable to every producer of wealth, if he would control his own industry, or make his labor most productive.

Consequently, it says, practically — so far as it is in its power to say — that only one person in four hundred of the population shall be permitted to have capital; or, consequently, to labor directly for himself; and that all the rest of the four hundred shall be compelled to labor for this one, at such occupations, and for such wages, as he shall see fit to dictate.

In short, the system says — as far as it can say — that only 100,000 persons — only one person in four hundred of the population — *shall be suffered to have any money!* And, consequently, that all the property and labor of the thirty-nine million nine hundred thousand (39,900,000) persons shall be under the practical, and nearly absolute, control of these 100,000 persons! It says that thirty-nine million nine hundred thousand (39,900,000) persons shall be in a state of industrial and commercial servitude (to the 100,000), elevated but one degree above that of chattel slavery.

And this scheme is substantially carried out in practice. These 100,000 men call themselves "*the business men*" of the country. By this it is meant, not that they are the producers of wealth, but only that they alone handle the money! Other persons are permitted to sell only to them! to buy only of them! to labor only for them! and to sell to, buy of, and labor for, them, only at such prices as these 100,000 shall dictate.

These 100,000 so called "*business men*," not only own the government, but they *are* the government. Congress is made up of them, and their tools. And they hold all the other departments of the government in their hands. Their sole purpose is power and plunder; and they suffer no constitutional or natural law to stand in the way of their rapacity.

How many times, during the last presidential canvass, were we told that "*the business men*" of the country wished things to remain as they were? Having gathered all power into their own hands, having subjected all the property and all the labor of the country to their service and control, who can wonder that they were content with things as they were? That they did not desire any change? And their money and their frauds being omnipotent in carrying elections, there was no change.

These 100,000 "business men," having secured to themselves the control of all bank credits, and thereby the control of all business depending on bank loans; having also obtained control of the government, enact that foreigners shall not be permitted to compete with them, by selling goods in our markets, except under a disadvantage of fifty to one hundred per cent.

And this is the industrial and financial system which the "National" bank system establishes — so far as it can establish it. And this is the scheme by means of which these 100,000 men cripple, and more than half paralyze, the industry of forty millions of people, and secure to themselves so large a portion of the proceeds of such industry as they see fit to permit.

CHAPTER IX.

AMASA WALKER'S OPINION OF THE AUTHOR'S SYSTEM.

As Mr. Amasa Walker is considered the highest authority in the country, in opposition to all paper currency that does not represent gold or silver actually on hand, it will not be impertinent to give his opinion of the system now proposed.

He reviewed it in a somewhat elaborate article, entitled " *Modern Alchemy,*" published in the *Bankers Magazine* (*N. Y.*) for December, 1861.

That he had no disposition to do any thing but condemn the system to the best of his ability, may be inferred from the following facts.

After describing the efforts of the old alchemists to transmute the baser metals into gold, he represents all attempts to make a useful paper currency as attempts *" to transmute paper into gold."* He says that the idea that paper can be made to serve the purposes of money is *" a perfectly cognate idea"* with that of the old alchemists, that the baser metals can be transmuted into gold. (p. 407.)

He also informs us that —

" It is perfectly impracticable *to transmute paper into gold* to any extent or degree whatever, and that all attempts to do so (beneficially to the trade and commerce of the world) are as absurd and futile as the efforts of the old alchemists to change the baser metals into the most precious." (p. 415).

These extracts are given to show the spirit and principle of his article, and the kind of arguments he employs against all paper that represents other property than coin; even though that property have equal value with coin in the market.

Yet he says : —

" One thing we cheerfully accord to MR. SPOONER's system — *it is an honest one*. Here is no fraud, no deception. *It makes no promise that it cannot fulfil*. It does not profess to be convertible into specie [on demand]. It is the best transmutation project we have seen." (p. 413).

When he says that "it is the best *transmutation* project he has seen," the context shows that he means to say that it *comes nearer to transmuting paper into gold*, than any other system he has seen.

This admission, coming from so violent an opponent of paper currency, may reasonably be set down as the highest commendation that *he* could be expected to pay to any *paper* system.

He also says : —

" Many schemes of the same kind have, at different times, been presented to the world; but none of them have been more complete in detail, or more systematically arranged, than that of MR. SPOONER. (p. 414).

But by way of condemning the system as far as possible, he says : —

" Mr. Spooner, however, can, we think, make no claim to originality, so far as the general principle is concerned. The famous bank of John Law, in France, was essentially of the same character." (p. 413.)

No, it was *not* essentially of the same character. One difference — to say nothing of twenty others — between the two systems was this : that Law's bank issued notes that it had no means to redeem ; whereas Mr. Walker himself admits that " Mr. Spooner's *system-makes no promises that it cannot fulfil.*" That is to say, it purports to represent nothing except what it actually represents, viz.: property that is actually on hand, and can always be delivered, *on demand,* in redemption of the paper. Is not this difference an " essential " one ? If Mr. Walker thinks it is not, he differs " essentially " from the rest of mankind. What fault was ever found with John Law's bank, except that it could not redeem its paper ? Will Mr. Walker inform us ?

www.ingramcontent.com/pod-product-compliance
Lightning Source LLC
Chambersburg PA
CBHW020253290326
41930CB00039B/1047